TREATS

just great recipes

GENERAL INFORMATION
The level of difficulty of the recipes in this book
is expressed as a number from 1 (simple) to 3 (difficult).

TREATS
just great recipes
spaghetti

McRae Books

Types of Long Pasta

Spaghetti is the classic long dried pasta shape and its name is synonymous with pasta itself in many parts of the world. But there are several other long pasta shapes, ranging in size from tiny cappellini, through the various widths of spaghetti, to the much thicker, and hollow, bucatini and ziti. Some long pasta shapes, such as linguine or reginette, are flattened, while others, like fusilli lunghi, are spiralled or curved. Some broader types, such as reginette, have fluted or scalloped edges.

Long pasta generally works well with smooth, olive oil based sauces that can be twirled around a fork. This book has 39 recipes for delicious sauces; we have indicated a specific type of long pasta to use in each recipe but almost all can be served with any long pasta with spectacular results.

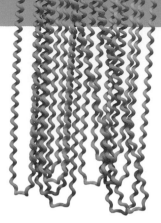

Fusilli lunghi

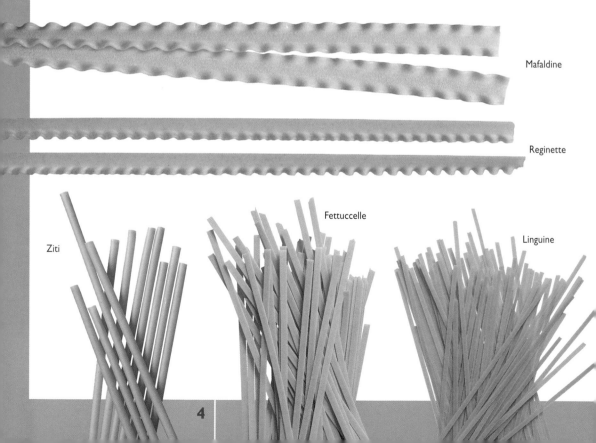

Mafaldine

Reginette

Ziti

Fettuccelle

Linguine

4

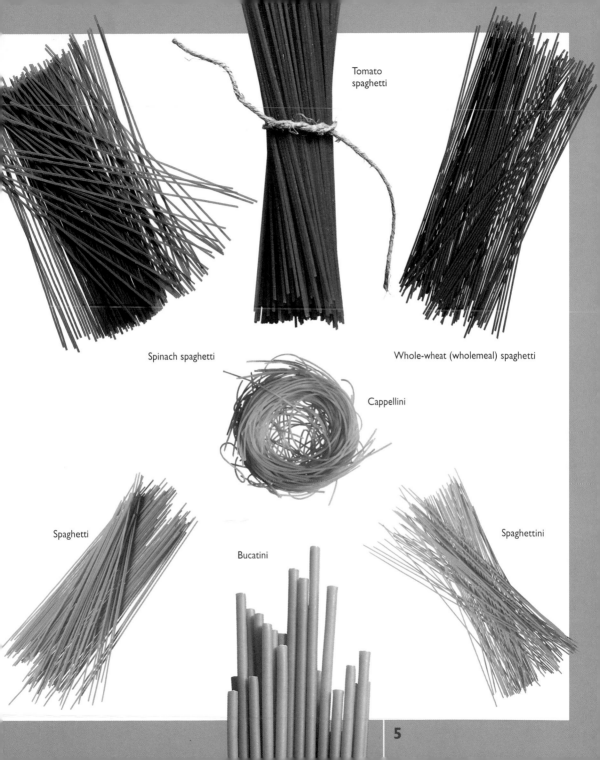

Tomato
spaghetti

Spinach spaghetti

Whole-wheat (wholemeal) spaghetti

Cappellini

Spaghetti

Spaghettini

Bucatini

5

Spaghetti
with asparagus

Bring a large pot of salted water to a boil over high heat. • Cook the asparagus in a large pot of salted, boiling water until tender, 5–7 minutes. Drain and chop, reserving 3 or 4 spears to garnish. • Heat the oil in a large frying pan over medium heat. Add the shallots and sauté until tender, 2–3 minutes. • Add the chopped asparagus and season with salt and pepper. Stir in the tomatoes and parsley. Simmer for 10 minutes, stirring from time to time, until the sauce thickens. • Meanwhile, cook the pasta in the boiling water until al dente. • Drain and add to the frying pan. Toss over high heat for 1 minute. • Sprinkle with cheese and garnish with the reserved asparagus. Serve hot.

- 1 lb (500 g) g asparagus spears, tough parts of the stems removed
- 1/4 cup (60 ml) extra-virgin olive oil
- 2 shallots, finely chopped
- Salt and freshly ground black pepper
- 1 2/3 cups (400 g) tomato passata (sieved tomatoes)
- 2 tablespoons finely chopped parsley
- 1 lb (500 g) spaghetti
- 1/4 cup (30 g) freshly grated mild Pecorino or other mild firm cheese

Spaghetti
with sun-dried tomatoes

Bring a large pot of salted water to a boil over high heat. • Heat the oil in a large frying pan over medium heat. Add the garlic and sun-dried tomatoes and sauté until the garlic is pale gold, about 3 minutes. • Add the canned tomatoes and cook until the sauce is thick, about 10 minutes. • Meanwhile, cook the pasta in the boiling water for 5 minutes. Add the green beans and cook until the pasta is al dente and the beans are tender. • Drain well and add to the frying pan with the sauce. Season with salt and pepper. Toss gently over high heat for 1 minute. • Serve hot.

¼ cup (60 ml) extra-virgin olive oil
3 cloves garlic, thinly sliced
3 oz (90 g) sun-dried tomatoes, soaked in warm water for 15 minutes, drained and coarsely chopped
1 (14-oz/400-g) can tomatoes, with juice, chopped
1 lb (500 g) spaghetti
12 oz (350 g) green beans, trimmed
Salt and freshly ground black pepper

SERVES 4–6

PREPARATION 1 h + 1 h to drain

COOKING 1 h

DIFFICULTY level 1

Spaghetti
with fried eggplant and tomato

Place the eggplant slices in a colander and sprinkle with the coarse sea salt. Let drain for 1 hour. Shake off as much salt as possible. • Heat the oil in a large deep frying pan until very hot. • Fry the eggplant in small batches until golden brown, 5–7 minutes per batch. • Drain on paper towels. • Tomato Sauce: Stir together the tomatoes, onion, garlic, basil, oil, sugar, and salt in a medium saucepan. Cover and simmer over medium heat until the tomatoes have broken down, about 15 minutes. • Uncover and simmer over low heat until reduced, about 40 minutes. • Transfer to a food processor and chop until smooth. • Meanwhile, cook the pasta in a large pot of salted boiling water until al dente. • Drain and add to the sauce. Toss well. Top with the fried eggplant and sprinkle with the Parmesan. • Serve hot.

1 large eggplant (aubergine), weighing about 1 lb (500 g), thinly sliced
2 tablespoons coarse sea salt
1 cup (250 ml) olive oil, for frying

Tomato Sauce
2 lb (1 kg) firm-ripe tomatoes, peeled and coarsely chopped
1 red onion, thinly sliced
2 cloves garlic, finely chopped
Leaves from 1 small bunch basil, torn
2 tablespoons extra-virgin olive oil
1/4 teaspoon sugar
Salt

1 lb (500 g) spaghetti or bucatini
1 cup (125 g) freshly grated Parmesan

Spaghetti
with walnut pesto

Cook the spaghetti in a large pan of salted, boiling water until al dente. • Pesto: While the pasta is cooking, chop the basil, garlic, walnuts, and pine nuts in a food processor. Gradually add the oil as you chop. • Transfer to a small bowl. Stir in the cheese and season with salt and pepper. • Drain the pasta and place in a heated serving bowl. • Add the pesto and toss gently. • Serve hot.

1 lb (500 g) spaghetti

Pesto
1 large bunch fresh basil leaves
2 cloves garlic
15 walnuts, shelled
3 tablespoons pine nuts
1/2 cup (125 ml) extra-virgin
    olive oil
Salt and freshly ground black pepper
1/2 cup (60 g) freshly grated
    Pecorino cheese

Spaghetti
with tomato sauce

Cook the tomatoes with the salt in a covered saucepan over medium heat for 5 minutes. • Transfer to a colander with large holes and let drain for 1 hour. • Return to the saucepan and add the onion, garlic, basil, oil, sugar, and salt. Partially cover and simmer over low heat until the sauce is reduced, about 40 minutes. • Remove from the heat and run through a food mill or process in a food processor or blender until smooth. • Cook the spaghetti in a large pan of salted, boiling water until al dente. • Place in a heated serving bowl and toss with the sauce. • Serve hot.

3 lb (1.5 kg) firm-ripe tomatoes, peeled and coarsely chopped

Salt to taste

1 red onion, thinly sliced

2 cloves garlic, finely chopped

Leaves from 1 small bunch basil, torn

2 tablespoons extra-virgin olive oil

$1/2$ teaspoon sugar

1 lb (500 g) spaghetti

SERVES 4–6

PREPARATION 15 min

COOKING 15 min

DIFFICULTY level 1

Spaghetti
alla carbonara

Bring a large pot of salted water to a boil over high heat. • Sauté the onion in the oil in a small saucepan over medium heat until lightly browned, 2–3 minutes. • Add the bacon and sauté until crisp, about 5 minutes. Remove from the heat and set aside. • Beat the egg yolks and cream in a large bowl. Season with salt and pepper and sprinkle with the Parmesan. • Cook the pasta in the boiling water until al dente. • Drain and add to the bacon. Return to high heat, add the egg mixture, and toss the briefly so that the eggs cook lightly but are still creamy. • Serve immediately.

1 onion, finely chopped
1/4 cup (60 ml) extra-virgin olive oil
1 1/3 cups (160 g) diced bacon
6 large eggs
1/3 cup (90 ml) heavy (double) cream
Salt and freshly ground black pepper
   to taste
3/4 cup (90 g) freshly grated Pecorino
   or Parmesan cheese
1 lb (500 g) spaghetti

Linguine

with tomato, olives, and chile

Bring a large pot of salted water to a boil over high heat. • Heat the oil in a large frying pan over medium heat. Add the garlic and sauté until pale golden brown, about 3 minutes. • Add the tomatoes and season with salt and pepper. Cook for 10 minutes, then stir in the capers and olives. Simmer until the tomatoes have broken down and the sauce is slightly thickened, about 10 minutes. • Cook the pasta in the boiling water until al dente. • Drain and add to the pan. Toss over high heat for 1 minute. • Sprinkle with parsley and chile powder and serve hot.

1/3 cup (90 ml) extra-virgin olive oil

4 cloves garlic, finely chopped

2 lb (1 kg) ripe tomatoes, peeled and coarsely chopped

Salt and freshly ground black pepper

2 tablespoons capers preserved in brine, rinsed and drained

1 1/2 cups (150 g) pitted black olives, coarsely chopped

1 lb (500 g) linguine

3 tablespoons finely chopped parsley

1/2 teaspoon chile powder

SERVES 4–6

PREPARATION 10 min

COOKING 30 min

DIFFICULTY level 1

Linguine
with spicy tomato sauce

Bring a large pot of salted water to a boil over high heat. • Heat the oil in a large frying pan over medium heat. Add the garlic and sauté until pale golden brown, about 3 minutes. Remove and discard the garlic. • Add the tomatoes and cook over high heat until the tomatoes begin to break down, about 25 minutes. • Add the chile pepper, Tabasco, and paprika. Season with salt, mix well, and remove from the heat. • Meanwhile, cook the pasta in the boiling water until al dente. • Drain and transfer to a serving dish. Sprinkle with the cheese. Add the sauce and toss well. • Serve hot.

1½ lb (750 g) ripe tomatoes, peeled and coarsely chopped

⅓ cup (90 ml) extra-virgin olive oil

2 cloves garlic, lightly crushed but whole

1 dried red chile pepper, crumbled

3 drops Tabasco sauce

1 teaspoon spicy paprika

Salt

1 lb (500 g) linguine

¾ cup (90 g) freshly grated Pecorino or Parmesan cheese

SERVES 4–6

PREPARATION 40 min

COOKING 2 h 10 min

DIFFICULTY level 1

Spaghetti
with meat sauce

Sauté the beef in the oil in a large frying pan over high heat until browned all over, about 5 minutes. • Add the onion, celery, carrot, garlic, rosemary, and 2 tablespoons of parsley and cook for 5 minutes. • Season with salt and pepper. Pour in the wine and let it evaporate. • Stir in the tomatoes and simmer over medium-low heat for at least 2 hours, adding stock as the sauce begins to thicken and stick to the bottom of the pan. • Remove the rosemary. • Just before the sauce is ready, cook the spaghetti in a large pan of salted, boiling water until al dente. • Drain well and toss with the meat sauce. • Serve hot sprinkled with the remaining parsley.

1½ lb (750 g) ground (minced) beef
⅓ cup (90 ml) extra-virgin olive oil
1 onion, finely chopped
1 stalk celery, finely chopped
1 carrot, finely chopped
2 cloves garlic, finely chopped
1 sprig fresh rosemary
3 tablespoons finely chopped parsley
Salt and freshly ground black pepper
½ cup (125 ml) dry red wine
4 large firm-ripe tomatoes,
    peeled and coarsely chopped
1–2 cups (250–500 ml) beef stock
    (homemade or bouillon cube)
1 lb (500 g) spaghetti

Spaghetti
with pancetta, mozzarella, and eggs

Place the eggs in a saucepan of cold water. Bring to a boil over medium heat. Cook for 8 minutes from the moment the water reaches a boil. Drain and cool the eggs under cold running water. Shell the eggs and chop them. • Heat the oil in a large frying pan over medium heat. Add the eggplants and sauté until tender, about 10 minutes. Use a slotted spoon to transfer the eggplants to a layer of paper towels. Let drain. • Add the garlic and pancetta to the frying pan and sauté until lightly browned, about 5 minutes. • Stir in the tomatoes and chile pepper and season with salt and pepper. Simmer over low heat until the tomatoes have broken down and the sauce is thick, about 30 minutes. • Meanwhile, cook the pasta in a large pot of salted boiling water until al dente. • Drain and add to the frying pan along with the mozzarella. Toss over high heat for 1 minute. Transfer to a serving dish. • Arrange the cooked eggplant on top of the pasta. Sprinkle with the chopped egg and serve hot.

2 large eggs
⅓ cup (90 ml) extra-virgin olive oil
3 small eggplants (aubergines), cut into small cubes
2 cloves garlic, finely chopped
4 oz (125 g) pancetta or bacon, chopped
2 (14-oz/400-g) cans tomatoes, with juice
1 red chile pepper, seeded and chopped
Salt and freshly ground black pepper
4 oz (125 g) fresh mozzarella cheese, drained and cut into small cubes
1 lb (500 g) spaghetti

Spaghetti
with oregano and anchovies

Bring a large pot of salted water to a boil over high heat. • Heat the oil in a large frying pan over medium heat. Add the garlic and sauté until golden brown, about 3 minutes. Remove and discard the garlic. • Add the anchovies and sauté—crushing with a fork—until dissolved into the oil, about 5 minutes. • Add the capers and oregano. Season with salt and pepper. Mix well and then remove from the heat. • Meanwhile, cook the pasta in the boiling water until al dente. • Drain, reserving 3 tablespoons of the cooking liquid. Add the pasta and the reserved cooking liquid to the frying pan. Toss over high heat for 1 minute. • Sprinkle with the cheese and serve hot.

⅓ cup (90 ml) extra-virgin olive oil

3 cloves garlic, lightly crushed but whole

8 anchovy fillets preserved in oil, drained

2 tablespoons capers, preserved in salt, rinsed, drained, and chopped

1 teaspoon dried oregano

salt and freshly ground black pepper

1 lb (500 g) spaghetti

½ cup (60 g) freshly grated Pecorino or Parmesan cheese

Spaghettini
with ricotta and pecorino

Bring a large pot of salted water to a boil over high heat. • Mix the fresh ricotta, butter, ricotta salata, chile pepper, and salt in a large bowl. • Cook the pasta in the boiling water until al dente. • Drain, reserving 2 tablespoons of the cooking water. Transfer the pasta to the bowl with the ricotta mixture, adding the reserved cooking water. • Toss well, sprinkle with Pecorino, and serve hot.

1 cup (250 g) fresh ricotta cheese, drained

1/3 cup (90 g) butter, cut up

1/2 cup (60 g) freshly grated ricotta salata cheese or other tasty aged grating cheese

1 dried chile pepper, crumbled

Salt

1 lb (500 g) spaghettini

1/2 cup (60 g) freshly grated Pecorino cheese

SERVES 4–6

PREPARATION 20 min

COOKING 20 min

DIFFICULTY level 1

Spaghetti
with summer vegetables

Bring a large pot of salted water to a boil over high heat. • Cook the green beans in a large pot of salted boiling water until tender, about 7 minutes. Drain well. • Cook the pasta in the boiling water until al dente. Drain well. • Transfer to a serving bowl and add 2 tablespoons of the oil. Toss well. • Add the garlic, green beans, celery, tomatoes, zucchini, bell pepper, arugula, the remaining oil, and the vinegar. Season with salt and pepper, and toss well. • Serve immediately.

5 oz (150 g) green beans, trimmed
  and cut in short lengths
1 lb (500 g) whole-wheat (wholemeal)
  spaghetti
$1/3$ cup (90 ml) extra-virgin olive oil
1 clove garlic, finely chopped
2 celery sticks, chopped
20 cherry tomatoes, quartered
3 small zucchini (courgettes),
  cut into julienne strips
1 yellow bell pepper (capsicum), seeded
  and cut into small squares
3 oz (90 g) arugula (rocket), chopped
1 tablespoon white wine vinegar
Salt and freshly ground black pepper

SERVES 4–6

PREPARATION 20 min

COOKING 20 min

DIFFICULTY level 1

Spaghettini
with mint, garlic, and olives

Bring a large pot of salted water to a boil over high heat. • Heat the oil in a large frying pan over medium heat until pale gold, about 3 minutes. • Add the anchovies and sauté—crushing with a fork—until they have dissolved into the oil, about 5 minutes. • Remove from the heat and add the mint and parsley. • Meanwhile, cook the pasta in the boiling water until al dente. • Drain and add to the sauce. • Sprinkle with the capers and olives, toss well, and serve hot.

2 cloves garlic, lightly crushed but whole

⅓ cup (90 ml) extra-virgin olive oil

3 anchovies, cleaned and finely chopped

2 tablespoons finely chopped mint

4 tablespoons finely chopped parsley

1 lb (500 g) spaghettini

2 tablespoons capers preserved in brine, rinsed

16 black olives, pitted and chopped

Spaghetti
with black olives and anchovies

Bring a large pot of salted water to a boil over high heat. • Sauté the onion and chile in the oil in a large frying pan over medium heat for 5 minutes. • Add the garlic and anchovies and sauté over low heat, crushing the anchovies with a fork until they have dissolved into the oil, about 5 minutes. • Stir in the tomatoes and simmer for 15 minutes. • Add the olives and capers and simmer for 5 more minutes. • Meanwhile, cook the pasta in the boiling water until al dente. • Drain and add to the sauce. Sprinkle with the parsley, toss well, and serve hot.

1/2 red onion, chopped
1–2 dried chile peppers, crumbled
1/3 cup (90 ml) extra-virgin olive oil
3 cloves garlic, finely chopped
4 salt-cured anchovy fillets
1 1/2 lb (750 g) ripe tomatoes, peeled and finely chopped
1 cup (100 g) black olives
1 tablespoon salt-cured capers, chopped
1 lb (500 g) spaghetti
1 tablespoon finely chopped parsley

SERVES 4–6

PREPARATION 10 min

COOKING 15 min

DIFFICULTY level 1

Ziti
with walnut pesto and cheese

Cook the pasta in a large pot of salted boiling water until al dente. • Drain the pasta over a large serving bowl, so that the boiling water heats the bowl. Discard the water, dry the bowl, and fill with one-third of the pasta. Cover with one-third of the pesto and cheese. Repeat until all the ingredients are in the bowl. Toss well. • Serve hot, garnishing each portion with a sprig of fresh basil.

1 lb (500 g) ziti, broken up into pieces
1 quantity pesto (see page 10)
1 cup (125 g) freshly grated Caciocavallo cheese or Provolone cheese
4–6 sprigs fresh basil, to garnish

SERVES 4–6

PREPARATION 10 min

COOKING 25 min

DIFFICULTY level 1

Spaghetti
with onion and tuna

Bring a large pot of salted water to a boil over high heat. • Heat the oil in a large frying pan over medium heat. Add the onion and sauté for until softened, about 5 minutes. • Add the water and stock cube. Mix well and simmer until the onion is transparent and very tender, about 5 minutes. • Add the tuna and mix well. Simmer until the sauce is slightly thickened, about 4 minutes. Remove from the heat and stir in the parsley. • Meanwhile, cook the pasta in the boiling water until al dente. • Drain and add to the frying pan. Toss over high heat for 1 minute. • Garnish with parsley and serve hot.

2 tablespoons extra-virgin olive oil
2 medium white onions, thinly sliced
1/4 cup (60 ml) water
1/2 vegetable stock cube
8 oz (250 g) canned tuna, drained and crumbled
2 tablespoons finely chopped parsley + extra sprigs, to garnish
1 lb (500 g) spaghetti

29

SERVES 4–6

PREPARATION 20 min

COOKING 35 min

DIFFICULTY level 2

Ziti

with artichokes and goat cheese

Bring a large pot of salted water to a boil over high heat. • Clean the artichokes by snapping off the tough outer leaves. Trim the stalk and cut off the top third of the leaves. Cut in half and use a sharp knife to remove any fuzzy core. Slice thinly. • Heat 2 tablespoons of oil in a large frying pan over high heat. Add the garlic and sauté for 1 minute. Add the artichokes and sauté until the garlic is pale golden brown, about 3 minutes. • Lower the heat, cover, and cook until the artichokes are tender, about 15 minutes. Add a little water if the artichokes begin to stick to the pan. • Add the parsley and mix well. • Toast the pine nuts in a small nonstick frying pan until pale golden brown, about 3 minutes. • Beat the goat cheese, pine nuts, salt, pepper, and half the cheese in a large bowl. Gradually stir in the remaining oil. • Cook the pasta in the boiling water until al dente. • Drain, reserving 3 tablespoons of the cooking liquid. Add the pasta and the reserved cooking liquid to the sauce and toss well. Add half the artichokes and their cooking juices. Top with the remaining artichokes. Sprinkle with the remaining cheese and serve hot.

1 lb (500 g) fresh artichokes
1/3 cup (90 ml) extra-virgin olive oil
2 cloves garlic, finely chopped
4 tablespoons finely chopped parsley
1/4 cup (45 g) pine nuts
14 oz (400 g) soft fresh goat cheese
Salt and freshly ground black pepper
1/2 cup (60 g) freshly grated Pecorino cheese
1 lb (500 g) ziti or other long pasta

Spaghetti
with tomato and cheese

Bring a large pot of salted water to a boil over high heat. • Heat the oil in a large saucepan over low heat. Add the onion and the garlic and sauté until the onion is softened, about 5 minutes. • Add the tomatoes and basil. Mix well, cover, and simmer over low heat until slightly reduced, about 30 minutes. • Stir in the cream, Fontina, and Gruyère. Stir until the cheese has melted and the sauce is smooth. Season with salt and pepper. • Meanwhile, cook the pasta in the boiling water until al dente. Drain well and transfer to a serving dish. Add the Parmesan and toss well. • Add the sauce and toss again. Season with a little more pepper. Garnish with basil and serve hot.

1/4 cup (60 ml) extra-virgin olive oil
1 large white onion, finely chopped
2 cloves garlic, finely chopped
2 (14-oz/400-g) cans tomatoes,
   with juice
12 leaves basil, torn + extra sprigs,
   to garnish
1/3 cup (90 ml) heavy (double) cream
2 oz (60 g) Fontina or other mild firm
   cheese, cut into small cubes
2 oz (60 g) Gruyère cheese,
   cut into small cubes
Salt and freshly ground black pepper
1 lb (500 g) spaghetti
1/2 cup (60 g) freshly grated Parmesan

Spaghetti
with marinated game sauce

Rinse the hare thoroughly and cut it into large chunks, taking care not to splinter the bones excessively. • Place the pieces of meat in a glass or ceramic bowl with the vinegar and water. Cover with plastic wrap (cling film) and let marinate in the refrigerator for 4 hours. • Drain the meat thoroughly and pat dry. • Heat the oil and lard in a large saucepan and sauté the meat over medium-high heat until browned all over, 8–10 minutes. • Add the onion, garlic, bay leaves, cinnamon, cloves, and rosemary and sauté for 3 minutes. • Stir in the wine and the tomato paste mixture. • Cover and simmer over low heat for at least 2 hours, or until the meat is tender, adding more water if the sauce begins to stick to the pan. (If you are cooking rabbit instead of hare, it will only take about 1 hour.) • Just before the sauce is ready, cook the pasta in a large pot of salted boiling water until al dente, about 12 minutes. • Drain and add to the sauce. • Toss well and serve hot.

1 young hare (or 1 rabbit), weighing about 3 lb (1.5 kg)

2 cups (500 ml) white wine vinegar

2 cups (500 ml) water + more as needed

1/4 cup (60 ml) extra-virgin olive oil

1 1/4 cups (150 g) diced lard or pancetta (or bacon)

1 large red onion, finely chopped

2 cloves garlic, crushed but whole

2 bay leaves

1 sprig rosemary

1 small stick cinnamon

2 cloves

2 cups (500 ml) dry red wine (use dry white wine if using rabbit)

1 tablespoon tomato paste (concentrate) dissolved in 3/4 cup (180 ml) beef stock

Salt and freshly ground black pepper

1 lb (500 g) spaghetti

SERVES 4–6

PREPARATION 15 min

COOKING 20 min

DIFFICULTY level 2

Linguine
with pesto, potatoes, and beans

Bring a large pot of salted water to a boil over high heat. • Cook the green beans in a pot of salted boiling water until almost tender, 3–4 minutes. Drain and set aside. • Cook the linguine in the boiling water for 5 minutes. Add the potatoes and cook until the pasta is al dente and the potatoes are tender, about 7–8 minutes more. • Drain well, reserving 3 tablespoons of the cooking liquid, and transfer to a large serving bowl. • Add the oil and the reserved cooking liquid to the pesto. Spoon over the pasta and potatoes, add the green beans and toss well. Season with pepper. Sprinkle with the Parmesan. • Garnish with basil and serve hot.

14 oz (400 g) green beans, chopped
1 lb (500 g) linguine
6–8 new potatoes, cut into small cubes
1 quantity pesto (see page 10, made without the walnuts)
3 tablespoons extra-virgin olive oil
Freshly ground black pepper
1 oz (30 g) Parmesan, cut into flakes
Sprigs of basil, to garnish

SERVES 4–6

PREPARATION 10 min

COOKING 15 min

DIFFICULTY level 1

Spaghetti
with garlic and bread crumbs

Bring a large pot of salted water to a boil over high heat. • Heat the oil in a large frying pan over medium heat. Add the garlic and sauté for 1 minute. • Add the bread crumbs and oregano and sauté until the bread crumbs have browned, about 3 minutes. Remove from the heat. • Cook the pasta in the boiling water until al dente. • Drain and add to the pan with the bread crumb mixture. • Toss over medium heat until the sauce sticks to the pasta, 1–2 minutes. • Season with pepper and serve hot.

½ cup (125 ml) extra-virgin olive oil
4 cloves garlic, finely chopped
3 cups (175 g) day-old bread, crumbled
2 tablespoons finely chopped
    fresh oregano or
    2 teaspoons dried oregano
1 lb (500 g) spaghetti
Freshly ground black pepper

SERVES 4–6

PREPARATION 10 min

COOKING 15 min

DIFFICULTY level 1

Spaghettini
with garlic, anchovies, and chile

Bring a large pot of salted water to a boil over high heat. • Heat the oil in a large frying pan over medium heat. Add the garlic and chile pepper. Sauté until the garlic is pale golden brown, 2–3 minutes. Remove and discard the garlic and chile pepper. • Add the anchovies and sauté for 5 minutes, crushing them with a fork until they have dissolved into the oil.. • Add the bread crumbs and parsley. Lower the heat and sauté until the mixture looks quite dry and crumbly, about 5 minutes. Remove from the heat. • Meanwhile, cook the pasta in the boiling water until al dente. Drain well and add to the frying pan. Toss well and transfer to a serving dish. • Garnish with parsley and serve hot.

1/2 cup (125 ml) extra-virgin olive oil
4 cloves garlic, lightly crushed
      but whole
1 red chile pepper, seeded
      and cut in 4 pieces
6 anchovy fillets
1 cup (60 g) fresh bread crumbs
2 tablespoons finely chopped parsley,
      + extra sprigs, to garnish
1 lb (500 g) spaghettini

SERVES 4–6

PREPARATION 40 min

COOKING 3 h 20 min

DIFFICULTY level 2

Spaghetti
with meatballs

Sauce: Sauté the onion and carrot in the oil in a large frying pan over medium heat until softened, about 5 minutes. • Add the beef and sauté,until browned all over, 8–10 minutes. • Add the tomatoes and season with salt. Simmer over low heat until the meat is very tender, about 3 hours. Remove the meat. It can be served separately after the pasta. • Meatballs: Mix the veal, egg, Parmesan, bread crumbs, and nutmeg in a large bowl until well blended. Shape the mixture into balls the size of marbles. • Heat the frying oil in a large frying pan. Fry the meatballs in small batches until golden brown, 5–7 minutes. Drain on paper towels. • Cook the pasta in a large pot of salted boiling water until al dente. • Drain and add to the pan with the sauce. Toss well with the meatballs and serve hot.

If preferred, make a quicker version of this traditional southern Italian recipe by replacing the sauce in this recipe with the simpler tomato sauces on pages 8 or 9.

Sauce
1 small onion, finely chopped
1 carrot, finely chopped
1/4 cup (60 ml) extra-virgin olive oil
12 oz (350 g) beef, in a single cut
2 lb (1 kg) ripe tomatoes, peeled and
    chopped
Salt

Meatballs
12 oz (350 g) ground (minced) beef
1 egg
2 cups (250 g) freshly grated
    Parmesan cheese
4 cups (250 g) fresh bread crumbs
1/4 teaspoon freshly grated nutmeg
1 cup (250 ml) olive oil, for frying
1 lb (500 g) spaghetti

SERVES 4

PREPARATION 5 min

COOKING 35 min

DIFFICULTY level 1

Spaghetti
with mushrooms

Bring a large pot of salted water to a boil over high heat. • Heat ¼ cup (60 ml) of the oil in a large frying pan over medium heat. Add the garlic and sauté until pale golden brown, about 3 minutes. • Add the mushrooms and sauté until tender, about 10 minutes. Season with salt and pepper. • Heat the remaining oil in a small frying pan over medium heat. Add the pancetta and sauté until lightly browned and crisp, 3–4 minutes. • Add the pancetta to the frying pan with the mushrooms. Mix well and sauté over low heat for 2 minutes. • Meanwhile, cook the pasta in the boiling water until al dente. • Drain well and add to the frying pan with the mushroom mixture. Toss over high heat for 1 minute. Add the parsley and season with pepper. • Sprinkle with freshly grated cheese and serve hot.

⅓ cup (90 ml) extra-virgin olive oil

2 cloves garlic, finely chopped

1½ lb (750 g) button mushrooms, sliced

Salt and freshly ground black pepper

8 oz (250 g) pancetta or bacon, cut into small pieces

1 lb (500 g) spaghetti

2 tablespoons finely chopped parsley

1 cup (120 g) freshly grated Pecorino or Parmesan cheese

Spaghetti
with lemons and black olives

Bring a large pot of salted water to a boil over high heat. • Beat together the oil, lemon zest, lemon juice, black olives, garlic, and basil in a large bowl. Season with salt and pepper. • Cook the pasta in the boiling water until al dente. Drain well and add to the bowl with the sauce. Toss well. • Transfer to a serving dish. Serve hot.

½ cup (125 ml) extra-virgin olive oil

Zest of 2 lemons, cut into julienne strips

Freshly squeezed juice of 2 lemons

1½ cups (150 g) pitted black olives, coarsely chopped

2 cloves garlic, finely chopped

16 basil leaves, torn

Salt and freshly ground black pepper

1 lb (500 g) spaghetti

SERVES 4–6

PREPARATION 1 h

COOKING 2 h 40 min

DIFFICULTY level 1

Fusilli lunghi
with meat sauce

Heat the oil and lard in a large saucepan over medium heat. Add the onions, pancetta, bay leaf, and beef. Cover and cook over medium-low heat for about 30 minutes, stirring often. • Increase the heat and pour in the wine and stock. Add the basil, parsley, salt, and pepper and bring to a boil. • Lower the heat and simmer, partially covered, for at least 2 hours, adding more stock if the sauce becomes too thick. • Cook the pasta in a large pot of salted boiling water until al dente. • Drain and add to the sauce. Toss well. Sprinkle with Pecorino and serve hot.

¼ cup (60 ml) extra-virgin olive oil
2 tablespoons lard or butter
2 onions, finely chopped
1¾ cups (200 g) diced pancetta (or bacon)
1 bay leaf
2 lb (1 kg) ground (minced) beef
⅔ cup (150 ml) dry white wine
⅔ cup (150 ml) beef stock, boiling + more as needed
Leaves from 1 small bunch basil, torn
1 tablespoon finely chopped parsley
Salt and freshly ground black pepper
1 lb (500 g) fusilli lunghi
6–8 tablespoons freshly grated aged Pecorino cheese

SERVES 4–6

PREPARATION 15 min

COOKING 30 min

DIFFICULTY level 1

Spaghetti
with vegetable sauce

Bring a large pot of salted water to a boil over high heat. • Heat the oil in a large frying pan over medium heat. Add the onions, celery, carrots, peas, and zucchini. Season with salt and pepper. Sauté until the onion is softened, about 5 minutes. • Add the tomatoes and mix well. Cover and simmer over low heat until the tomatoes have broken down and the sauce is slightly thickened, about 20 minutes, • Meanwhile, cook the pasta in the boiling water until al dente. • Drain and add to the frying pan. Toss over high heat for 1 minute. • Transfer to a serving dish. Sprinkle with the Parmesan and serve hot.

1/4 cup (60 ml) extra-virgin olive oil
2 large onions, finely sliced
6 celery sticks, finely chopped
2 medium carrots, finely chopped
1 cup (150 g) frozen peas
2 medium zucchini (courgettes),
    cut into small pieces
Salt and freshly ground black pepper
1 (14-oz/400-g) can tomatoes,
    with juice
1 lb (500 g) whole-wheat (wholemeal)
    spaghetti
1/2 cup (60 g) freshly grated Parmesan
    cheese

Reginette
with pine nuts and raisins

Bring a large pot of salted water to a boil over high heat. • Heat the oil in a large frying pan over medium heat. Add the garlic and sauté until pale gold, about 3 minutes. • Add the pine nuts and raisins and sauté until the pine nuts are golden, about 3 minutes. • Stir in the tomato paste mixture. Add the anchovies and stir with a fork until they dissolve into the oil, about 5 minutes. • Season lightly with salt and a generous grinding of pepper. • Meanwhile, cook the pasta in the boiling water until al dente. • Drain, reserving 2 tablespoons of the cooking water. Add to the sauce with the reserved cooking water. • Toss well, sprinkle with the parsley, and serve hot.

2 cloves garlic, finely chopped
$1/2$ cup (125 ml) extra-virgin olive oil
4 tablespoons pine nuts
4 tablespoons golden raisins (sultanas)
$1/2$ cup (125 ml) tomato paste (concentrate) dissolved in $1/2$ cup (125 ml) water
8 anchovy fillets
Salt and freshly ground black pepper
1 lb (500 g) reginette
2 tablespoons finely chopped parsley

SERVES 4–6

PREPARATION 30 min

COOKING 45 min

DIFFICULTY level 2

Spaghetti
with mantis shrimp

Wash the shrimp and remove the eyes. Cut open the bellies with kitchen scissors. Use a teaspoon to remove the flesh. Place in a large bowl and set aside. • Fill a large saucepan with cold water, season with salt, and add the shrimp shells. Boil for 20 minutes, then strain the stock. • Sauté the garlic in 2 tablespoons of butter in a large frying pan over high heat until pale gold, 1–2 minutes. • Add the shrimp flesh and simmer for 5 minutes. • Pour in the wine, season with salt, and remove from the heat. • Cook the pasta in the strained stock until al dente. • Drain, reserving 2 tablespoons of the stock. Add the pasta and the reserved stock to the frying pan. • Dot with the remaining butter, letting it melt into the pasta. Sprinkle with parsley and serve.

3 lb (1.5 kg) mantis shrimp, such as cicale (canocchie) or substitute regular shrimp or lobster

Salt

3 cloves garlic, finely chopped

1/3 cup (90 g) butter, cut up

1/4 cup (60 ml) dry white wine

1 lb (500 g) spaghetti

2 tablespoons finely chopped parsley

Spaghetti
with radicchio and cheese

Bring a large pot of salted water to a boil over high heat. • Heat the oil in a large frying pan over medium heat. Add the onion and sauté until softened, about 5 minutes. • Add the radicchio and mix well. Lower the heat, cover and cook until the radicchio is tender, 5–7 minutes. Season with salt and pepper. • Meanwhile, cook the pasta in the boiling water until al dente. • Drain well and add to the frying pan with the radicchio. Add the cream, Fontina, and nutmeg. Toss over high heat for 2 minutes and serve hot.

¼ cup (60 ml) extra-virgin olive oil
1 large onion, thinly sliced
5 small heads of radicchio, shredded
Salt and freshly ground black pepper
1 lb (500 g) spaghetti
½ cup (125 ml) heavy (double) cream
8 oz (250 g) Fontina or other mild firm cheese, cut into small cubes
½ teaspoon freshly grated nutmeg

Spaghetti
with bell peppers and pancetta

Bring a large pot of salted water to a boil over high heat. • Heat the oil in a large frying pan over medium heat. Add the pancetta and sauté until lightly browned, about 3 minutes. • Add the onion, garlic, parsley, basil, and bell peppers. Sauté until the bell peppers and onions are tender, about 10 minutes. • Stir in the tomatoes, chile pepper, and oregano, and season with salt. Mix well, cover, and simmer over low heat until the tomatoes have broken down, about 15 minutes. • Add the capers and olives. • Meanwhile, cook the pasta in the boiling water until al dente. • Drain and add to the frying pan. Toss over high heat for 1 minute. • Sprinkle with the freshly grated cheese and serve hot.

1/3 cup (90 ml) extra-virgin olive oil

3 oz (90 g) pancetta or bacon, chopped

1 large onion, finely chopped

1 clove garlic, finely chopped

2 tablespoons finely chopped parsley

6 basil leaves, torn

2 red bell peppers (capsicums), seeded and finely sliced

2 yellow bell peppers (capsicums), seeded and finely sliced

1 (14-oz/400-g) can tomatoes, with juice

1/2 red chile pepper, seeded and chopped

1/2 teaspoon dried oregano

Salt

2 tablespoons capers preserved in brine, rinsed and drained

Handful green olives, pitted and coarsely chopped

1 lb (500 g) spaghetti

1/2 cup (60 g) freshly grated Pecorino or Parmesan cheese

Bucatini

with olives and mushrooms

Bring a large pot of salted water to a boil over high heat. • Heat the oil in a large frying pan over low heat. Add the parsley and garlic and sauté until the garlic is pale gold, about 3 minutes. • Stir in the lemon juice, olives, chile pepper, and anchovies. Stir with a fork over low heat until the anchovies dissolve into the sauce, about 5 minutes. Season lightly with salt and generously with pepper. • Cook the pasta in the boiling water until al dente. • Drain, reserving 3 tablespoons of the cooking water. Add the pasta and the reserved cooking water to the frying pan. Toss over high heat for 1 minute. • Serve hot.

1/4 cup (60 ml) extra-virgin olive oil

6 tablespoons finely chopped parsley

3 cloves garlic, finely chopped

Juice of 1/2 lemon

1 cup (100 g) pitted green olives, coarsely chopped

1 dried chile pepper, crumbled

4 anchovy fillets preserved in salt, rinsed and chopped

5 oz (150 g) mixed wild mushrooms preserved in oil, drained and chopped

Salt and freshly ground black pepper

1 lb (500 g) bucatini

SERVES 4–6

PREPARATION 20 min

COOKING 25 min

DIFFICULTY level 1

Spaghettini
with tomato fish sauce

Bring a large pot of salted water to a boil over high heat. • Sauté the garlic in the oil in a large frying pan over medium heat until pale gold, about 3 minutes. • Stir in the tomatoes and cook over high heat until the tomatoes have broken down, 10–15 minutes. • Add the fish and season with salt and pepper. Cook for 5 minutes, shaking the pan. • Discard the garlic and remove from the heat. • Cook the pasta in the boiling water until al dente. • Drain and add to the sauce. Toss over high heat for 1–2 minutes. Sprinkle with the parsley and serve hot.

2 cloves garlic, lightly crushed but whole
1/2 cup (90 ml) extra-virgin olive oil
2 lb (1 kg) tomatoes, peeled and finely chopped
1 lb (500 g) g small fresh fish, such as sardines, whitebait or anchovies
Salt and freshly ground black pepper
1 lb (500 g) spaghettini
2 tablespoons finely chopped parsley

Linguine
with seafood sauce

Bring a large pot of salted water to a boil over high heat. • Cut the squid bodies into small chunks and slice the tentacles in half. • Heat the oil in a large frying pan over high heat. Add the garlic and sauté until pale gold, 1–2 minutes. • Add the squid, jumbo shrimp, crayfish, and shrimp and cook over medium heat for 5 minutes. • Cook the pasta for half the time indicated on the package in the boiling water. • Drain and add to the sauce. • Pour in the wine, season with salt, and cook, gradually adding the fish stock and mixing occasionally until the pasta is al dente. Season with salt and serve hot.

1 lb (500 g) squid or cuttlefish, cleaned
2 cloves garlic, finely chopped
1/2 cup (125 ml) extra-virgin olive oil
6 shrimp (prawns), shelled, leaving the head and claws on
6 jumbo shrimp or king prawns
6 crayfish, shelled, leaving the head on
1 lb (500 g) linguine
1/2 cup (125 ml) dry white wine
Salt
6 cups (1.5 liters) fish stock, boiling

SERVES 4–6

PREPARATION 30 min + 1 h to soak

COOKING 25 min

DIFFICULTY level 2

Spaghetti
with clams and mussels

Soak the clams and mussels in a large bowl of cold water for 1 hour.
• Drain and rise well under cold running water. Scrub or pull any beards off the mussels. Place in a large saucepan, add 4 tablespoons of the wine, and cook over high heat until open, 5–10 minutes. Discard any that do not open. Remove about half the shellfish from their shells. • Strain the cooking liquid and set aside. • Bring a large pot of salted water to a boil over high heat. • Sauté the garlic and chile pepper in the remaining oil in a large frying pan over medium heat until the garlic is pale gold, about 3 minutes. • Add the clams and mussels (both shelled and unshelled) and cook for 2 minutes. • Pour in the remaining wine and cook until it evaporates. • Meanwhile, cook the pasta in the boiling water until al dente. • Drain and add to the sauce, adding a little of the strained cooking liquid from the clams. • Toss with the butter and sprinkle with the parsley. Serve hot.

1½ lb (750 g) clams, in shell
1½ lb (750 g) mussels, in shell
⅔ cup (150 ml) dry white wine
4 cloves garlic, finely chopped
½ teaspoon dried chile pepper
⅓ cup (90 ml) extra-virgin olive oil
1 lb (500 g) spaghetti
2 tablespoons butter, cut up
2 tablespoons finely chopped parsley

SERVES 4–6

PREPARATION 20 min + 1 h to soak

COOKING 30 min

DIFFICULTY level 2

Spaghetti
with spicy clam sauce

Soak the clams in cold water for 1 hour. • Bring a large pot of salted water to a boil over high heat. • Put the clams into a large pan over medium heat with a little water. Cook until they open, 5–10 minutes. Discard any clams that do not open. Remove from the heat and discard most of the clam shells. • Heat the oil in a large frying pan over medium heat. Add the garlic and chile pepper and sauté until the garlic is lightly browned, about 3 minutes. • Add the tomatoes and wine, season with salt, and cook until the tomatoes begin to break down, about 15 minutes. • Add the clams and stir well. • Meanwhile, cook the pasta in the boiling water until al dente. Drain and add to the pan with the clams. Toss over high heat for 2 minutes. • Sprinkle with parsley and serve hot.

2 lb (1 kg) clams, in shell
$^1/_3$ cup (90 ml) extra-virgin olive oil
4 cloves garlic, finely chopped
1 red chile pepper, seeded and chopped
5 ripe tomatoes, cut into segments
$^1/_3$ cup (90 ml) dry white wine
Salt
1 lb (500 g) spaghetti
3 tablespoons finely chopped parsley

SERVES 4–6

PREPARATION 30 min + 1 h to soak

COOKING 30 min

DIFFICULTY level 1

Linguine
with mussels

Soak the mussels in a large bowl of cold water for 1 hour. Pull or scrub off any beards. • Bring a large pot of salted water to a boil over high heat. • Pour ½ cup (125 ml) of wine into a large saucepan and cook the mussels over high heat, shaking the pan occasionally, until open, 5–10 minutes. Discard any that do not open. • Remove most of the mussels from their shells. Leave some in the shells to garnish. • Sauté the garlic, chile, and parsley in the oil in a large frying pan over medium heat until the garlic is pale gold, about 2 minutes. • Pour in the remaining wine and let it evaporate. • Add the tomatoes and simmer over medium heat until they have broken down, about 15 minutes. • Season with salt. • Add the mussels and cook for 5 minutes more. • Meanwhile, cook the pasta in the boiling water until al dente. • Drain well, add to the sauce and toss well. Serve hot.

4 lb (2 kg) mussels, in shell
¾ cup (180 ml) dry white wine
2 cloves garlic, finely chopped
1 fresh red chile pepper, finely chopped
1 tablespoon finely chopped parsley
⅓ cup (90 ml) extra-virgin olive oil
3 lb (1.5 kg) firm-ripe tomatoes, peeled and coarsely chopped
Salt
1 lb (500 g) linguine

SERVES 4–6

PREPARATION 30 min + 1 h to soak

COOKING 40 min

DIFFICULTY level 2

Baked seafood
Spaghetti

Soak the clams and mussels in a large bowl of cold water for 1 hour. • Drain and rise well under cold running water. Scrub or pull any beards off the mussels. • Remove the mottled skin from the squids and cut the bodies into small chunks. Cut the tentacles in half. • Preheat the 350°F (180°C/ gas 4). • Sauté the garlic, chile, and parsley in the oil in a small saucepan over high heat until the garlic is pale gold, about 3 minutes. • Pour in the wine and let it evaporate. • Add the tomatoes and cook for 10 minutes. • Add the squid, clams, mussels, and crayfish. Cover and simmer over medium heat until the clams and mussels open up. • Remove from the heat and discard any clams or mussels that haven't opened. • Shell half the seafood. • Cook the spaghetti in a large pot of salted boiling water for half the time indicated on the package. • Drain, reserving the cooking water, and add to the seafood sauce, tossing well. • Cut 4–6 large pieces of aluminum foil and fold each one in half to double the thickness. • Divide the pasta into 4–6 portions and place in the center of the pieces of aluminum foil, adding 3 tablespoons of cooking water from the pasta to each portion. Close, sealing the foil well. There should be an air pocket in each of the packages. • Bake until the parcels have puffed up slightly, 12–15 minutes. • Serve the foil parcels directly on the table.

1½ lb (750 g) clams, in shell
1½ lb (750 g) mussels, in shell
14 oz (400 g) small squid, cleaned
2 cloves garlic, finely chopped
1 dried red chili pepper
2 tablespoons finely chopped parsley
⅓ cup (90 ml) extra-virgin olive oil
½ cup (125 ml) dry white wine
1½ lb (750 g) firm-ripe tomatoes, peeled and chopped
12 oz (350 g) shelled crayfish
1 lb (500 g) spaghetti
Salt